of

form

&

gather

2004, *Pity the Drowned Horses*, Sheryl Luna
Final Judge: Robert Vasquez

2006, *The Outer Bands*, Gabriel Gomez
Final Judge: Valerie Martínez

2008, *My Kill Adore Him*, Paul Martínez Pompa
Final Judge: Martín Espada

2010, *Tropicalia*, Emma Trelles
Final Judge: Silvia Curbelo

2012, *A Tongue in the Mouth of the Dying*, Laurie Ann Guerrero
Final Judge: Francisco X. Alarcón

2014, *Furious Dusk*, David Campos
Final Judge: Rhina P. Espaillat

2016, *Of Form & Gather*, Felicia Zamora
Final Judge: Edwin Torres

The Andrés Montoya Poetry Prize, named after the late California native and author of the award-winning book, *The Iceworker Sings*, supports the publication of a first book by a Latino or Latina poet. Awarded every other year, the prize is administered by Letras Latinas—the literary program of the Institute for Latino Studies at the University of Notre Dame.

# of form & gather

FELICIA ZAMORA

UNIVERSITY OF NOTRE DAME PRESS

NOTRE DAME, INDIANA

University of Notre Dame Press
Notre Dame, Indiana 46556
www.undpress.nd.edu

Published in the United States of America

Library of Congress Cataloging-in-Publication Data

Names: Zamora, Felicia M., author.
Title: Of form & gather / Felicia Zamora.
Other titles: Of form and gather
Description: Notre Dame, Indiana : University of Notre Dame Press, [2017] |
    Series: The Andres Montoya poetry prize
Identifiers: LCCN 2016053423 (print) | LCCN 2017000658 (ebook) | ISBN
    9780268101787 (softcover : acid-free paper) | ISBN 0268101787 (softcover :
    acid-free paper) | ISBN 9780268101794 (pdf) | ISBN 9780268101800 (epub)
Subjects: | BISAC: POETRY / American / General.
Classification: LCC PS3626.A6278 A6 2017 (print) | LCC PS3626.A6278
    (ebook) | DDC 811/.6—dc23
LC record available at https://lccn.loc.gov/2016053423

∞ This paper meets the requirements of ANSI/NISO Z39.48-1992
(Permanence of Paper).

for Chris . . . as always, you know why

The growing presence of the butterfly in her
Does not fill her with fear. . . .

And this world inside another, larger cocoon.
                    —Aleš Šteger, *The Book of Things*

All day long I feel created.
                    —Annie Dillard, *Holy the Firm*

We value that droning inner voice. . . .

—I cannot see.
What ascension
in things? I ask

                    —Sally Keith, *design*

Contents

in in; gather gather

To be out of—dually other

Acknowledgments

Thank-you to the editors of the following journals and presses in which these poems first appeared, sometimes in different forms:

The Adirondack Review, "Distinct Separation Felt"

BOMB, "The America Gap"

The Burnside Review, "Sower"

The Cincinnati Review, "In tuck"

Columbia Poetry Review, "In extant" and "This lure"

Cutbank Literary Journal, "In still"

Hotel Amerika, "This tug" and "Of ghosts"

Indiana Review, "Decoy"

Juked, "Book of the Robin in the Bird: II. Primative Streak"

Meridian, "& in wonder too"

Notre Dame Review, "Same river"

Phoebe, "No Fisher"

Pleiades, "Book of the Robin in the Bird: VI. Allantois dries— the chick uses her own lungs"

Poetry Northwest, "Continuous Non-Replication"

Salt Hill, "Con-Form"

Third Coast, "In fasten-nation"

TriQuarterly, "In practice" and "Fallible Roundness"

West Branch, "Not not" and "In outline"

Witness, "In middle with other," "O for Passage," and "Peel-Back"

The following poems were first published in a chapbook-length publication in *Verse* as winner of the 2015 Tomaž Šalamun Prize:

"Where you find yourself"
"Physics of where we stand"
"To know little"
"In patterns"
"In the breast of"
"Drift"
"To begin"
"& wings made of matchsticks"

Thank-you to Letras Latinas at the University of Notre Dame's Institute for Latino Studies for creating and supporting Latinos in poetry with the Andrés Montoya Poetry Prize. Thank-you to the University of Notre Dame Press.

I am forever grateful to Edwin Torres for selecting my manuscript and allowing these poems a chance to speak to the world. I am honored.

Warm thanks to my mentors and dear friends, Stephanie G'Schwind and John Calderazzo, your encouragement, time, and listening ears have meant the world to me.

Much love to Mel and Joe for your constant belief in me and support. We've always had each other, which allows for magic.

Thank-you to my mother for planting the seed; I love you.

Deepest appreciation to my partner, friend, and confidant, Chris. You hear my poems over and over again with honest patience. Your unwavering advocacy for my poetic life and your love keeps all this alive. You are my person, my love, and my inspiration.

Introduction to the Poems

With its measured and continual revelation, Felicia Zamora has crafted a work that celebrates form as human evolution—the poem's breath, the poet's body—passing over time in a landscape thirsty for passage.

In *Of Form & Gather*, poems become choral assemblages to their proximity, tuned into the maker's spirit as coiled out from unhurried interactions with ancestral zygotes. Where does identity invoke place over silence—intimate implications of nuance, trust in the reader's ability to move in concert with the writer's soul? If even a fraction of beyond-space is gleaned by possibility, the maker's job is done. If one could imagine what awaits between where one could go and why one has remained, would that bring us to a finite completion—a cyclic undercarriage of removal in the language remaining?

Zamora's reminder is to affect each part of the poem by implementing a profoundly gentle humanity that connects to the shifting external across borders, continuously returning to invention with a charge to the "think," a dare to the heart, that allows movement in the ubiquity of silence. In a sort of volcanic empathy with spirits invoked by the sling of creation across centuries borrowed and replanted. A poem's burden is to live inside its creation, where the organized singularity of its gathering is what brings the reader to the reader's own voice.

We are a culture redefined when we step into the culture that defines us—to expose its incomparable reach with the breath that moves us, with our body's volumetric rhythms shifting among our human matter. To own that geo-shift, to bring about *other* as *in*, to affect change by knowing that change needs to happen beneath layers of cognition, underneath our organized paradigms.

This is quietly revolutionary work that throws a gauntlet to the social diaspora. A living palimpsest to newly awaken our social engagement by breathing in a simultaneity of opposing forces—as tectonic plates of hearing that create fissures inside the unfolding kinetic.

If my job is to shepherd the reader through new terrain, let me introduce you to the lungs between the lines—the breathing of an object formed as one continuous vertebration—page to page, word to other. My obligation is to get out of my own way, to allow the work in its bio-syntactic intensity to speak quietly, without introduction or promise.

So I'll leave you with this: the ability to chart your course through your own questions is a human trait that you have the obligation to nurture. To wondrously allow your capacity for travel and enlarge your perception of a world continuously expanding, in whatever direction you choose. Read this work, look about you, and take a breath. We don't often have moments that bore deep and give back. Thank-you, Felicia, for giving us that opening.

—Edwin Torres,
Judge

circles
&
circulations

Where you find yourself

Droplets decorate the pane; what clouds
carry, storm in their chests; disobedient sky
rotates axis into light; east's promise of
dusk & muddles of middle

bide time in our retinas, make us

afford fleeting; strip you of garden, of plot
of ability to *plant* anything; your hands in
wet soil, womb of; say *seed*; say *connection gifts
you*—something heals

in the dark, in knowing the bright departs
& returns, brings lightening you cup your
hands to ears for. One fallen petal ebbs
ina puddle between showers. *Do you feel
lapping?* On your back

you see mirrors above, see mirrors below.

To know little

Behind partitions, where work unfolds you
desire *soul* here, yet frontal lobe pushes the
idea back. How itemized in our colloquial
manner/isms

as if brick and fluorescents remind our

bodies of anything other than *made made
made*. When thunder mystified & rainbows
schemed about us. Our minds patient &
moment laden

swanling deceived: separate from water.
The fowl innately feels flight, takes a mate
& swims with the same bill, same plumage
day after day

to carry a wingspan, folded on the lake.

Distinct Separation Felt

Roots of this cottonwood surface the ground & mimic trunk's stretch to sky; how we all in/out of something; how we all hint *hint hint*; when you say *firmament* you mean *vault of*, & heaven is a semicolon; aren't we all in distinct separation felt between clauses? Insert your mental picture of what lives in your heaven here _____; dash looms so awkward & watchful; it's the *watch* that makes it all so full. & in the full-full we reach for: unbreathable dark behind the blue; in utero first we gulp liquid; we of oxygen, reacquaint; space of us; quickly, we long to press our footprint; the dying stars laugh; the dead stars heavy & silent, long to laugh at the dying; & so this witness goes out & out; think *pebble in pond*; think *no no no*; think *all caterpillars contain a butterfly or moth*; think *you in a ball in float of space;* think *what powers you now*; & what do we really know about makers & un-doers? The caterpillar rolls into a ball;   already cocoon & soar sewn inside.

Continuous Non-Replication

& first days happen in equal cycles:
equinoxes, solstices, & all things that
remind us of *round round round*; aren't we all
in spin on the same ball

let's just say we give her a mother's name

let's just say *she* when we mean *otherly* & *us
but not us;* because what isn't circling inside
us that also isn't circling outside us? & so it
goes with both theory & prayer

in need, because *time* suggests *need.* & the
rose blooms, full head, & bows in weight;
your finger in prick of stem; & wounds &
feel; that hurt & beauty are synonymous,
but never one in the same; even the first

circle traces a new, over & over to its liking.

In the breast of

she keeps a cabinet of wood, chips of paint;
a thing reclaims more of. She removes
hinges, exposes the belly of shelves; speaks

what held in years beyond 100; & number

she hits with tongue atop the roof of her
mouth over & over until her palate tastes
the count. A maudlin carving of *Anna*
tattoos the door's shoulder

someone knew of journey—her fingers scan
the body in haunt of more; treasures in
reformation; to fall in; to bring history;
archways in all their daunting forms; haul
& wonder

at arms in wrap of girth, at hollow.

Of ghosts

You take a photo of the thermometer
outside the window; think *degrees of*; think
what blurs & what melts from; the truck full;
the tin roof gleams in midday

& her eyes in pools; think *torn of*; think

vacant; how the ditch overgrows & the table
once held rhubarb pie & asparagus picked;
think *an old highway*; think *a gravel lot*; think
three young hearts; think *play-*

ground; how we memory out of; how place
haunts behind each pupil; how rusted poles
suspend the *MOTEL* sign; shadows in cast;
think *spells*; cradle of; of the mulberry tree;
think *where fireflies catch*; bark once in curve

to your body, towers silent, deep in root.

Fallible Roundness

You open, wing-like & one-sided. How halves make the smirk & you always two things gathering. *Together*, repeats you. Opposites never really dance on ends; instead, this infinite loop, which goes on without us, because our anatomy knows of circles & circulation; & when we say *infinite*, or trace our clever little ovals kissing, we know we don't mean *human*. Loops tend to end with something in the body attacking, think *misbehave*, a giving up, twisted ___, a failing, cancer-this/cancer-that, smashing metal, a taking, smashing glass, & the list, in fact, goes on in meaningless ways in which words struggle to line-up, end to end, ironically, in domino fashion, to be knocked down by the inability to label all possibilities. This fallible roundness tunnels me to you. I remain in ellipsis at your ribcage; peer in the vast; hug these bone-bars; scribble path that weaves ventricles & times pumps; long for a *whole*, a tremor, oblique.

In layer

The heron expands; in two flaps, crosses
the lake & perches on a middle patch of
land; think *form* & *forming*; how sense
overtakes animal, reaction

& shadow of wingspan glides water

mirrors & pools—what each body brings
in motion with; we long to think *depth &
under*, yet a layer of layer, think *rings of a core*;
think *three dimensional latitude/longitude*

& our coordinates found in the under
folds of flesh, in curve of molar, in joint of
spine; how many pieces we in scene? Learn
to witness or witness to learn? Think *lake
view*; think *through the fish's*

eye; *ah*, we overtaken, watch the bass leap.

In fasten-nation

How drought forgets the face of rain staves
longing by the innate *know* of wet's return.
Ebb of *before*; ebb of *soon* & where of your
chest, weary in cycle? Doubt

inspires the child to bait her own line

What if? fishes in her pupils as she watches
her grandfather's delicate fingers pinch
worm. & we all fasten: hook to rhythms of
sea, or trail rocks in soles, or collection

of people—desperate to say *friend*, or
moment when dawn first pales the night,
you wake heart-full, astonish in swell
between your ears & a nameless melody
courses, stream-like, in your pores.

You recall not a single word; no; no need.

The America Gap

All the accolades of peace; in pretend; peace in races; the race for peace; yesterday President Obama said the n-word on a podcast in a garage; Marc Maron *hazy in the mind*; how a mind may seem powerless in this nation of space & words; Obama speaks of old haunts & *the books you need in five years*; a street once lived; journals & law; brave comfort; brave enough to say & not use. A confederate flag shackles to a pole in South Carolina; guns, guns; & you are? you are? *Where you come to peace?* & the difference between peace & struggle; a church where the hinges scream & think think; what we know of innocence— count to nine; people in slaughter over color; life over; & a flag with a message deeper than the Mississippi; hear ghosts in outrage: down, down to the shores where rivers supply & destroy simultaneously; rivers of sound waves; rivers of words, say *not enough to feel bad*; rivers of wounds; laws to regulate/not regulate: rivers of use/not use.

Italicized direct statements from the President Obama podcast on WTF June 22, 2015.

Prank

Duck's feet paddle air & a feathered
bottom bobs; underneath the wet, beak
busy in dive; how we all half unseen

instinct, half comical vaudeville for other;

say *what a show* & clever mouth mis-tells the
joke & laughter punches your line; lips
form *lemon* but the mind thought *Spicer's tree*
sentences back; how we all *slip*

slip; how process & consciousness love one
another, yet, prank on each other's door
steps; our necks in swivel, swivel &
through a two-way mirror, what scenes
given from the light; & in the dark—

fingers held in front of your eyes, in splay.

This tug

& the spider web waves, both delicate love & not love, from the officiator's microphone at the wedding: how we're all smirk-fully aghast & out of place. The man on the bike path chats with hands & mouth at only himself. What decision makes to hold/not hold? We're all talking heads—quiet in our cage of bone, if only to another's ear. Once, I was the redbreast-part of the robin; now I am mold under the board; your toes trounce so gentle, gentle so. When youthful, I sang of *sixpence* & believed my mind in draw of a small gather of colorful birds, plumage all shapes and sizes; now I just want to believe. Keep the coins for *rigor* & *mortise*, when peoples across the world make similar gestures in joining for similar the one act we *alone, alone, alone*. What we speak *of* does not speak of us. & so goes obsession of; once I was the orange rind; now I am the chicken-juice on the hand & the hand in wait of wash. Set anything side by side & emerges this tug.

Con-Form

Where the shore crumbles, cliff remains;
tree roots expose; da Vinci's Vitruvian
Man; we all in proportion to something
other; pull anything out of

dark gives the light place; think *purpose*;

to invert; to know the ruse of stagnant;
think *capture capture*; think *to draw what the
mind draws*; to fail collection; how paper
wanes & we all subject of time; think

lovely skeleton; dissect you down; to study
from the open; think *wound*; to cure, but we
only speak of meat; to dazzle in what the
lake chews away; to be spit out; what
consumes; gradually

erasure; to revive in the absence of.

that that that;
this this this

In stage

How you throw away—peeler handle unglued & unable to purpose; what happens when the things we think we know fail us? Has time just consumed as time eventually consumes? You in the mirror with a face you forget belongs to you; & now, stranger, how

old seeds without permission we all in subject of lines in dig

across the tendrils of brain in compact of—say *collect*, say

torn from a vine, a vine & flesh wears this life, permeable. In moment, a kitchen; now the knife, dull, chunking away—*carrot carrot carrot* & how you witness the girl in carry of two hands full of slender orange with leafy-green & pumpkins & patches & October grey; hay in your nostril; all things autumnal memorying, as if to . . .

Peel-back

How land lays over itself, sediment-full; we all in the belly of
something other; you witness the neighbor's dog in taunt of blue
day; this *just out of* & reach is a noun no longer in roll off your
tongue; how *arms-length* means *at bay at bay*; what you try to keep

out despises & the reflection of your bones in the mirror

means exposure; & you feel so *orange* in the peel-back

rinds of elbows, of knee caps; & wounds & their wide-wide-open,
if able, any locked door . . . & arches & more knobs; neighbor's pit
bull; foam in the mouth; when you compact it all down: a
mountain; who counts in landscapes? You ask a question & the
question stares back, blank, in dare to answer.

In still

& in conjure we learn intimate molecules heap in design to this
wide open, let's all stammer as we say *everything*, word of worlds;
both wide & otherwise; word in thalamus caught in kingdoms of
air, thought, & ink requires all & nothing of science

to build inside a body/outside a body; we all in string to;

lamps of energy burning & in burn.

To be peasant of language; to draw breath & what exhales paints
us; a *new* new; say *swaddle;* how the petal devotes to flower as flower;
how in night, first, you hear the leaves release from the aspen; how
the whisper devours you, unable   in sun's westerly crawl to forgive
the light, when you, *yes you*, in still,   in still.

O for passage

To know seasons by shadows, hawk breath, the dip of day early &
not early; a page exists for each of these; this too; as in sky, it's all
happening at once & you wonder how to hold a drop of rain
outside the wet; all these puzzles with no solutions & nothing to

puzzle in to or out from; you remember your cells

belonging to others, before the dark grew you

of flesh in weave, of veins in form; to incubate; to taste world in
liquid first; to know sky as your creator's belly; feel the continuous
hug of organs in soak; a haunt before womb; these months too a
season; a swarm of molecules & atoms in bind; & in float, a spark;
& an O for passage; mouth in gape before the tongue learns—

Promise

Half the aspen in the yard mourns the death of the other half;
something alive still, out of bereft sensation of bark; how we all
that that that; then *this this this*; something smells of sky in the rain;
the child traces her lips with a pudgy finger & smiles in deep   deep

acknowledgement; what traces & leaves behind;

what light left on the eyelids after *flash flash*

flash; how instant & old this gather toward; say *infinitude*; say *place
beyond the forest*; say *the rot in your bones*; say *one leg in, one leg* well you
know; how rational & irrational this moment after birth; to not
remember something of us not in deterioration; the child licks her
lips after touch; promise to make; promise to keep.

Book of the Robin in the Bird

(Or Chick Embryo Development)

I. All the cells look alike

Something to be said of thirds: what to remember, what to forget; the human mind recalls like rhythm & rhyme & story; a gray area exists here & there & there & *gray area* is a colon with a billion blank lines behind it; gravitation pulls all mass toward & when caught in trajectory, Einstein calls this *relativity*; she begins in cull from others; third child of a house full of motion; house in tire of newness, in tire of dependence; & so the child grows with mulberries in her hair, presses knees to gravel, bends ears to the cricket's forewing; the forest loves her & she the forest; her thoracic cavity fills with acorns; her small hands dig dirt from the hillside—fort where she watches sheep roam.

II. Primitive Streak

Here, her head & backbone develop: on pavement, chain-link-every-thing, whistles, & finite ticks of the second hand between arithmetic & square pizza; where letters form sharp, piercing tools; knuckles bleed & the lips that speak *dirty spic*, bloat in purple hues; someone added *play* to this ground, idyllic & perhaps a bit ignorant; the absence resonates in the throats roaring in scene; yes, she finds herself seen—burning match among the dormant book, face both darker & ablaze; the squint of his eyes; more words; she in swell; then her boot between his legs; fists & fists to cheek bones & more fists; the circle engulfs her; some-where in the blur, in distance, a bell rings.

III. Elsewhere the heart forms

She circulates from two distinct systems; to think & to act; how this per-
meability of everything she's made up of; love in flashes; of what, she
cannot synthesize; her heart forms outside of her: stranger's motion &
faces & flesh in constant state of heat; she first rubs her clitoris on couch
arms when her mother's back turns; preacher warns *masturbation is a sin*;
she swings her legs in pews & dreams of dark hair & lips of the boy three
aisles forward; what a god knows & her body not shame, only quiet &
tender where muscles & fatty tissues verge to action, deep between her
legs, deep in brain tendrils where *desire* floats in the air above her; balloon
distending in fill, in fill.

IV. & buds of wings

Her body turns 90 degrees; what she knows of skeleton: elongation &
speed in her knees; she sees boundaries in the tree lines, cages in stalks
of corn; what isn't a barb wire fence to hop? Everything *flight flight flight;*
she envies the dandelion florets in dry; to be swept; to be carried in pur-
pose; her chest a field, in long of gust; her mind a cavern, still in tunnel;
how she waits; her heart knocks at her breastbone, longing for tenancy;
her mouth whispers *no no* in fear & capture is a form of servitude she
doesn't understand; she runs over & over until the gravel road meets
horizon; yet, her shadow stretches back, even in starlight, a tether sewn
inside.

V. Feather tracts & hatch

Almost visible to herself; how she wears her body, the fit close enough
to fool those who do not look close; look close now; she swallows her
heart & it perches behind ribs, makes home in a cage & desires song
above all; above all, a cerebral cortex nestles in, she wants to say *skull*,
but appropriateness pauses her—she in preparation; she tires of shells
of casings; she goes to college; she fucks & works long hours; she asks
big questions; she studies poetry; she finds *careers* not jobs & no one be-
lieves she doesn't want to rule the world; she only pretends for the sake
of pretending, boredom offends her; she feels her hips, her breasts, her
neck—all this to become; of what, of what . . .

VI. Allantois dries—the chick uses her own lungs

She speaks of eggs, of what's in the benedict sauce; she speaks in raw things; she rarely regurgitates for those who squirm; windows are windows; every so often, she throws a brick into glass; what *shatter* really resembles; she paints by numbers using only black & tips of her elbows crease with fate lines meant for palms; belief in cards, not decks; prayers to chaos, when chaos isn't looking; she winds her body in thread—to sew & tether; the flesh in hold; she reads the pamphlet in the seat back pocket; count to only one mask; to fasten; to *really* fasten; how choice burrows in; to pull instinct out, to show it around, give it the bottom bunk, steal its lunch money.

in in;
gather gather

In patterns

Take the columbine; five within five
corollas colorful & bowing. Sing a song of
doves in huddle. You know what names of
Latin give

hue of change to come. In spur length,

diversity beyond lips in cortexes in
shape/reshape of cells—dramatic these
morphological anythings when in focus
relevant taps the circumference of pupil

a dilation of landscape swallows inside; say
organ; say *how gather gather gather*; say *flower
flowers design so stamen, so rare* & yet the field
spreads of petals . . .

how harvest a thing requires   to &

Sower

What doesn't grow in a garden: hair & nails & bits of humanity; what we think makes up humanity; we never left; say *apple, apples, eat the apple;* Eden found still in elbow joints, in the high pitched ringing often in your ears. What is delicate & unfurling seeds from something delicate & unfurling; you think you lack a green thumb; the green in your thumb lacks none; listen to the growing in your veins; say *vines;* say *clever, no;* say *plant of the sun;* shake your head, what sprawl/crawl resembles. Knees in the dirt & zucchini leaf on your palm, resist the urge to just keep digging; the hole leads only to another hole in the same garden; to tend; to be tended; your mother calls you *little bean;* yes, a language exists for this too; a plot of; a sectioned part of; no plan, just overgrowth & weeds in strangle of. We draw an outline of farmer; see how your head, her head, our heads all fit into the shadow of straw; maker in the made; sower in the sown.

In middle with other

& the three butterflies lightly suspend just
above the road, knee high; flutters of six
wings, in almost embrace; what we think
we know of instinct; aren't we all in hover

& slightly out of place, bringing a bent

kind of beauty with us in our gait; *show me*
what your gait looks like? I'll show you mine.
Contrasts of yellows & oranges in delicate
bob against asphalt—something

necessary & at work here; where concrete
winds, so too, winds the work of insect; say
my thorax of me, my speckled body; say *I wonder*
in air & find you in pause, in witness; we all in
the middle with other, round & round

until whatever limbs we have tire {of} us.

In tuck

We hear the whistle in the distance & think *in constant lumber; this motion we belong to; this railway bone* & urge to jump on anything with a door for a belly to catch; how fast carries enough. Think *far far*, then rethink *what locomotion looks like*. We all along the side of tracks, our small amounts of everything bundled to a stick. The rest, well, *rest*. To the inbound we must take; what place we bring with us; that which grinds down molars & leaves scars. Think *the barb wire on your shins*, think *the mulberries in your hair*, both in tear of you, just so; how moments tuck in cerebral cortex, in fade among the tissues we too gave name. & in the whistles we tether the deep deep cells & transport & lyrics of melody in long forget & smell, full in your throat, of sheep's wool, a week before the sheer & cold light of the firefly abdomen; what lures us. Think *mason jar*, think *your small hands in capture*; think *humidity of summer's dark*; think *you, arms wide, in field of yellow glow*.

This lure

Dragonfly over lake; to view the reservoir
from middle; how the lap unravels edges
into view; when we speak of wings & fins,
do our words jealous in the lack of

forms in all the ubiquitous blueprints? Say

we carve from; say *wing forgot me*; build keels—
for float roams in spinal cord; build
gunwales—for our lungs forget water; &
we boat & boat

our lives in hull away from stern &
starboard; in fear of capsize; in distant
desire; to be water & not; to witness the
dragonfly; to lack hover; to be body in sink
at sight of the bank; say *this fade,*

this lure; an incantation from inception.

Not not

Bumblebee against asphalt; we all carry
contrast in our gait; to open a door & find
not a room at all, instead a grove of orange
trees & how

in our mouths nothing rhymes with *orange*

& outside our mouths nothing rhymes
either; & so goes obsessions with contours;
say *design*; think *Frost's white moth*; say *me me;*
think *if only*

this heart drew collages, stills of; to be child &
not; to let landscape witness you; to find a
lighthouse not yours; to make it so; to
unravel with desire; any skeletal part of; &
to notice bees in odd places, not

not a simple bee; to invert wonder; partake.

In extant

& the hummingbird enters torpor; what
brings us to *almost*; what must return from
body's slow trance; to understand keep;
how the spider crawls up the jaw

& dips one thin leg in the mouth,

withdraws & keeps saunter; to be in
familiar pastures; in extant; to know
regardless of; the heart pumps in manage
of wings beating one to fifty in a second;

say *metabolic*, say *what burns*, say *a lovely use of*,
& we all distant & watchful of our nature
in show; to peer out of fullness of mind,
eye forward; to catch the universe
unfolding at a fleshy-seam, say

expose, pupil hollow in design, in passage.

& in wonder too

Just overhead, a hawk; a hawk so close I trace the delicate designs & patterns of an open wingspan with my pupils; a hawk with a prairie dog flailing in talons; what does anyone know really about beauty? When young, I wrecked a dirt bike with my brother; slid down three-fourths of a hill on bare legs; think *all smiles & wind throughout*; think *what tear of flesh sounds like*; he held my chin, *don't look down*. Even now, the asphalt still in fuse to my knee; pale blue under the sheen of skin; scar tissue twists in tributaries; a small river built in me; & in wonder too beauty peeks just below. My mother eats frozen cherries; bags of frozen cherries; the acidity cracks & sores the creases of her mouth; with sores she eats cherries; cherries until her jaw bogs from pain; wonder her/e; think *how something simple & cellular & storied*; think *shush shush*; think *deep red against her pale*; think *hawk or prairie dog?* Story of you, cherry; or you, chin; or you, eyes of the prairie dog, wild.

In outline

In inlet of lake, we paddle slow boards over
a fallen tree; to sink but only so; to bend
what we think should not bend; to feel
mirrored

in one direction with end, in one direction

without end; & say *sky*; only mean *universe*;
think *heaven heaven*; & words combined with
thought conjure an odd type of magic &
our frontal lobe synapses

always half in & out of something. Tree
limbs in soak, until, think *piece by piece by*
what do we really know of disintegration?
The dust on your sill is mainly you; mourn
not what you leave behind; an outline

under a vague transparency for witness.

Same river

Consider the bank in constant wear,
constant erosion; what water does to one;
what water in one does; water *water* say *no
don't*, clever; consider how we all begin

lap or land? Perhaps the alluvial bits

of river bed, floating in & out of
definitions, carry secrets in their bellies; &
all the women's wombs—secret *secret*; say
human, what have you threading;

say *in your cranial?* Say *tendrils;* say *wave, wave;*
say *place where drowning lulls;* we approach the
river with intention; river shows us flow &
steeple of forest & where to kneel; our cells
in pull to the wet

& rush; the same river runs in—*yes, speak it.*

In practice

Cool sweeps over the streambed lip, say *here & here*, then, bare ankles in hug; these intimate moments at dusk; what dissipates; what stands in the place of *gone* when the jaw, in gape, remains a restless *O*, & wide to tunnel inward; say *incessant just beyond the thalamus*; blackness of the cat perched atop a railcar illuminates & the long strips of day in peel—how appropriately October inside the mind, & now too, season; all organic, all shift here; your eyes mid-swallow of shadow & temperature knocks at the base of your spine; how we all *in in* & *this* you now aware; of spots, specter forms & un-forms before you—small bodies in tumble one over other—gnats in swarm—to be a limb of need; to attach, belong to a larger; hold your breath & say *anything*; hold your breath: tiny wings in flap on your cheek, lip, in your hair; synapses of brain; chatter beyond your eardrum; type of prayer in flesh; say *realign*; realign in practice.

In spell

How we all spore of light-less space; secrets
cast in secret places; what the womb
resembles before you; not empty in wait;
say *speak first from fluid;* your throat a cave

& air & air your first gasps; to form

tangible a thing from our mouths; bound
in oxygen; say *specter,* say *the tongue in bend, in
trace, with breeze of our lungs;* & yet, magic in
syllables & tonality

in pitch & scale; a letter born of the jaw
fastens to another; say *this string of
incantations we use* & say *incantations* in
demonstration of; hear you now in conjure
of this line in read

ink of mind, in collaboration of.

To begin

Speck of cottonwood floats & destination
rules nothing in breeze; you long to pack
bags, head south, drive your car until the
radiator steams & desert & river & dune

dune dune; the approaching silence

in heavy concerto; the orchestra billows
with soloist & solos; part of a part of a fail
of sum; transistor, who knew you before
radio? & what kills the stars

a lack of inverted necks; pin-pricks in
boxes & dreamers in need of method. If
you trace anything back to origin—more
trails, more fingerprints, more quiet notes
hanging on lines of pages

in wait of instrument, a baton in lift.

To be out of—
dually other

Decoy

I am the ocean bottom; my craters full of bioluminescence twinkling in heavy, heavy dark. Who speaks of the float circling inside them? Cut open a creature; what do you expect? A line of labels & a thing exposed; think *clever me, let's slice an eel, pare down parts, see how we mean.* Now you, eel under knife. Now me. Hold the blade, away from anything that tears, cull the power of light, of adaptation, the fish in heavy wet with a glowing lure on its head; *that's something.* Do you need to collect all parts to be something? When first you swim, flesh remembers amniotic everything; you on the other hand, ignore the innate sense of fluidity. When I say *you* I mean *I*; a little I/Thou never hurt as long as you fasten *other's* oxygen mask first; I am a giant tube worm, plume scarlet; think *hemoglobin*; think *what carries in presence of sulfide*; think *insides I wear out*; & you consider *float*; the decoy made of bob & shine & teeth & fins & & &

Physics of where we stand

You draw a line; the top of the aspen
resembles a pitchfork, leaves quaking
green fire & we all contemplate death
separately; internal

dialogue rolls ticker-taping the mind out

& hibernation is less lifestyle choice than
instinct. You bring yourself to the wide
open page & the page bullies you back. The
line never empties, only

a string of lights & colors bouncing off each other;
inertia *inertia;* in wait for the act upon;
matter: always seeing demons in the trees.
I long to be your property of force; to
reference nothing political; you turn

from me divided: face half shadow, half.

No Fisher

So you're a fisherman? Strange phrases from strangers. You by the lake with a box. The thought of *tackle*; of hoist & lower, this system in levers. What you didn't catch, releases you. What you did catch, releases you; always a thing baiting for. So many forewarnings in retrospect. The whale in the sand does not resemble the whale in your mind. To be out of; two-realms; dually other. The whale in your mind spins on axes, out of water, 3-D, fully puffed & bloated to full whaleness. Your mind knows full whaleness requires water, salt, & depth—yet disobeys; your mind knows not all the anatomical parts, yet knows what is *not whale*. Your heart: a whale on land, sunken, containing the vision you knew of it, boxed & discombobulated. The sun's quiet chap on your lips, just so, to remind. Ubiquity culls at the bones. & this is not the ocean. So many forewarnings. & you, no fisher here. What you bring before all bodies of: questions & a box.

Drift

Attend to the cranial side of your ear drum,
who speaks to who? Voice in the box; utters
behind; space thickens & mind *becomes
becomes becomes*—then

fleck in distance; failing capture; you drift

restless vertebrae, flesh in elongation,
witness sun pull the blanket of twilight over
head & give night one last gaze. Sweet
gesture in repeat; repeat

this moment & *that moment* linger under each
lid wipes the eye, wipes the eye; all swept in
conversation. Of body & landscape, speak
of *keepers*, roll the *e*'s in your jaw. Taste *keep*

in capture, how *place* dwells inside.

& wings made of matchsticks

Interrupt, mid-flap. Erase *ablaze*, once fire catches. No red-tipped heads left to count; all singe; all dust. *What's left to cremate when the spirit hollows in fall?* You trace the stony bone that refuses to burn. Only the sun's magnetic love harvests elements sewn deep in grooves of your molars. You taste flight in porous regions, hidden from spark & flame—rhythm etches in undersides, in absence: this ash of heart thinks to re-beat & we're all convective motion, in sprawl . . . in sprawl.

Before caught; before your lips devour
only light: an elm sapling sprouts from
your ribs & you almost postpone flight.
Roots tempt you, graze your soft tissues
& whisper seeds in your wrists & ankles.
To lade you in the wet; make womb of
dark spaces; *promise*—Do you believe in
mostly hydrogen? No matter. Plasma
rethinks you; tethers your blood to the
central star. When her face turns pale, she
cloaks herself with giants. You, dear
whisperer, forget, forget, forget.

& here lies a sea even heavens fear.
Dolphin sings: the sonic muse; the fluke
propels in physicality, only, a brain
intelligent & cetacean. To remove wet; to
affix upon; to study outside of what
makes a porpoise a porpoise. We all
earthly & unearthly. Crawl from warmth,
molecules in bind of reformation. You
pause to think of gods here. *In an image,
of?* If we stare at the sun too long, do our
eyelids not coat red when closed? The
deep color making & making.

What of this winged nature; thought-caught in a loop of soar? Breastbone breaks to become passerine; an ever return to eaves; generation after generation—built nest, aerial feed. Vassal of air. You bring *home* with you; mimic hollows of sea anemone: a vessel during in between. To envelop the wind; desire the climb, climb until lungs threaten burst. This something tapping inside: how we dream eyes up, bathed in bright & pray eyes closed, limitless in direction.

& in chasing horizon, this rolling never-
fall. In middles, we swaddle in womb,
peregrine bloats in pelvis; layers nesting.
Even perennials yawn out of the same
root—original & babe-like, distinguished
by anthesis & time. *The lilac of the lilac bush
is not the lilac of the lilac bush that once was.*
Open the matchbox. *You are?* Look. Look
closer still. One head in burn smells of
the burn of many. Sliver matches into
four, hollow them out: fuse as bones.
Find a cliff. Tuck the collum in glide.

To be borne of no true jaw. *Who sang you before hatch?* Doused in lightness air carries the weight of beak; how beak becomes air. Rostrum from which melody hinges. You tear from mother incubating & alone. One of a clutch, you rest in a pocket of grass, mud & twigs high in branches. You tear from shell disobedient & dream-full: visions of dawn & equinox specter outside a calcium carbonate crib. You leave your youthful tooth beside the amniotic egg, chipped & purpose-full.

Inside your muscular chest, a wishbone. *Hope* sewn up in evolution. Dissect yourself, in gentle stride—*flight*, also, dwells in bones & actions. Are you not the sparrow-shadow you see above the meadow? How the pupil swallows light, for the mind to regurgitate pictorially. We refract: the lovely art of bending. Once you see the sparrow-shadow, is it not part of you . . . burnt upon the retina; captured inside tissues & tendrils of brain? There now, witness blueprint & design in form.

With faces of puddles, they chant, *Flight forgets you*. Demons borne at your ear rip wings from the blades of your back; in soft tide of utero, you first learn grief for the anatomy of birds. So begins your obsession with aeriform. Caught between liquid & air, once amniotic fluid filled you; child of angel, shaman wove a story for you & never drew back the veil—how angels sprout from frontal lobes & heavenly travels of hydrogen & helium in slumber west each night, in dream.

You read the story of Icarus as you bind together wings of matchsticks. To be *of fire* when the burn engulfs you—a true sense of approaching fountainhead; at first, you fear the flame; the bleat escapes your throat, smoke rising from fresh spark, & the fiery particle dwells in sack, collects moments of you in beat. Your chest a furnace: *the fire of you.* Your bleat designed of shepherd, returns you to ash, to bed you in the heavens with elemental gods; where *wax* & *hand-mades* fail.

& twilight forgets your face, wipes you in
lover's moonlight; how sun gives beyond
her hours of climb. Daughter of—Eve:
another daughter, another daughter on
fire in story. To all who tempt. To all who
speak to snakes, who reach for apples,
who lay in the grasses unware of
nakedness, who dream to construct
forelimbs of birds to join ancestors aloft
sky. Tell a story of you. Bathe your frail
outline in oblique refraction; illumination
harbors you; keeps limitless vigil.

In method, our blueprints permeate genomes & *cells*—interstices of our fabric stitch minute part to minute part. What of all these smallest units of life, replicating inside, independent & gorging? Army of you. Army for survival/arrival. Loop back to *becoming*. To be in a state *of . . . of* requires space; a *before* & *after*, space for cessation & regeneration. Oh, Hooke, how we see the unit of self: a monastery where monk dwells; monk where monastery dwells; faith an intimate loop, stirring tenet.

& when we say *anatomy*, do we not whisper *structure* in the brain? We, lovely animal. If we dissect ourselves down, may we add flight, skeleton deep? Silly mammal. Your hair smells of match, lit. Dragonfly hovers you in draft of hindwing & forewing. You know now, to harbor flight in the wind-blown sac where the heart once sat keeps you faithful, keeps belief of body & a reunion of your cells to the heat of the first cell. Drawn. You, moth. Drawn.

To wallow in belief: the echo approaches the echoer ... unable to return home. Head in the cave; the study of bats; if we invert our bodies enough; rushes & intonation of what chants inside; to the dark we find vision; to be mammal & webbed & capable of. Once, you floated in your own wet sky, amniotic & drowning in host. Always in tempt, you seek weightlessness; scent of lilac upon the air, a thing in carry; stone in pluck from riverbed, dries beside the bank & yearns in promise of cast.

In delicate bind, we seek questions to answers strung in fibers throughout our cells. You, dear reader, compose of cells *not human at all*: bacteria, archaea, methogens . . . what you carry inside, carries you. Microorganisms of wetlands, producing marsh gas, swirl in your gut. Picture paints the picture. We were made to be *made up of.* Let us swathe ligature of tatters & answers, build a new vessel we call *body* & toss bundle off cliffs in synchronicity in prayer.

To mold & be molded from. When were we no longer children playing with sticks? To create fire implies nothing of being *of fire*. When did sticks contort, refigure to metal & gasoline? How far from . . . these nests built inside you. Say *cranium*; say *that muscular organ sitting in sac*. Shake your head while you speak. Say *throne*. Fallen & fallen. You unpack vocabulary, let letters tumble from your jaw; you stand in a landscape of words, words in borrow, in break, in mend; what *wield* looks like.

& how the page, before you, blots back
vision with presence of all colors. Closer,
in reflection, maker? Harsh & soft light,
in simultaneous flux. It's not that nothing
exists first; instead the fullness consumes
& requires speech: *a hue completely
desaturated . . .*

                              & then, void of all
awakes—absorbing & love-full. Dark
how you carve out—sweet wound; ablaze.

About the Author

Photo by Joe Zamora

Felicia Zamora won the 2015 Tomaž Šalamun Prize from *Verse* and authored the chapbooks *Imbibe {et alia} here* (2016) and *Moby Dick Made Me Do It* (2010). Her published works may be found or forthcoming in *The Adirondack Review, The Cincinnati Review, Columbia Poetry Review, Crazyhorse, Hotel Amerika, Indiana Review, Meridian, Michigan Quarterly Review, The New Guard, The Normal School, North American Review, Phoebe, Pleiades, Poetry Daily, Poetry Northwest, Puerto del Sol, Tarpaulin Sky Magazine, TriQuarterly, Tupelo Quarterly, Verse Daily, West Branch, Witness,* and others. She is an associate poetry editor for the *Colorado Review* and holds an MFA in creative writing from Colorado State University. She lives in Colorado with her partner, Chris, and their two dogs, Howser and Lorca.

CPSIA information can be obtained
at www.ICGtesting.com
Printed in the USA
FFOW05n0715270117